WEATHER
AND CLIMATE

Design	David West Children's Book Design
Editorial Planning	Clark Robinson Limited
Picture Researcher	Emma Krikler
Illustrator	Ian Moores
Consultant	Barry Parker Meteorologist

© Aladdin Books 1991
Designed and produced by
Aladdin Books Ltd
28 Percy Street
London W1P 9FF

First published in
Great Britain in 1991 by
Franklin Watts
96 Leonard Street
London EC2A 4RH

ISBN 0-7496-0596-0

A CIP catalogue record for this book is
available from the British Library.

Printed in Belgium

HANDS · ON · GEOGRAPHY

WEATHER AND CLIMATE

DAVID FLINT

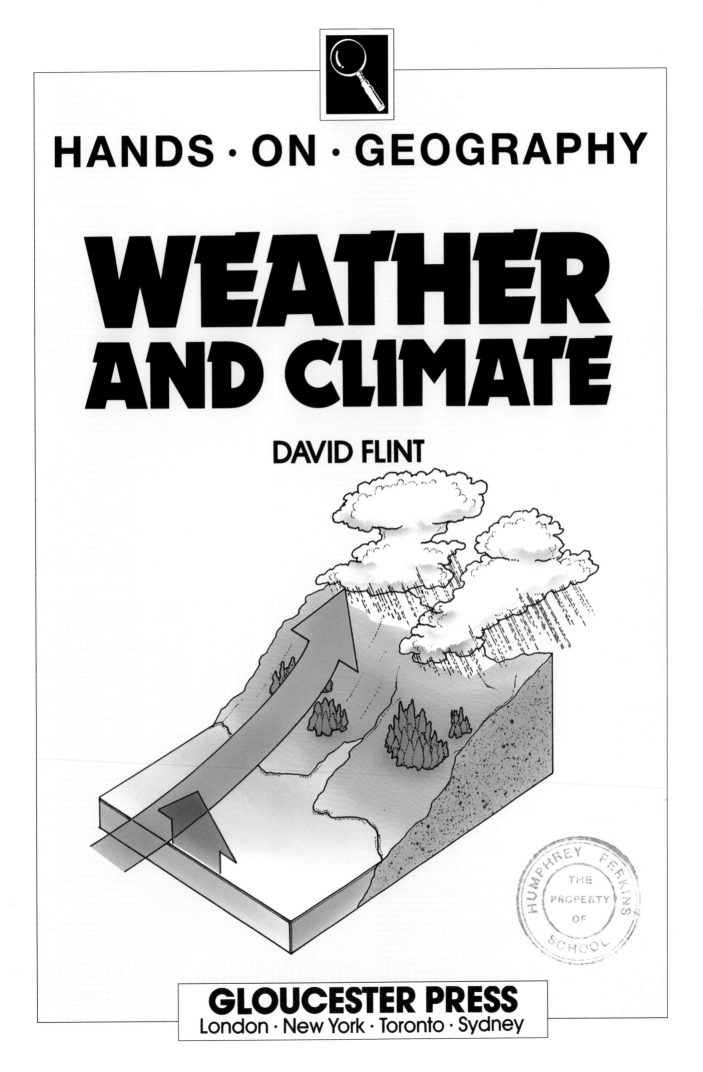

GLOUCESTER PRESS
London · New York · Toronto · Sydney

CONTENTS

This book concerns itself with weather and climate. The topics covered range from general trends in weather that affect us from day to day to the various climates that influence whole areas of the world. The book tells you about the different elements that make up the weather, how they change and the problems involved in trying to forecast the weather. There are "hands on" projects for you to do which use everyday items as equipment. There are also "did you know?" panels of information for added interest.

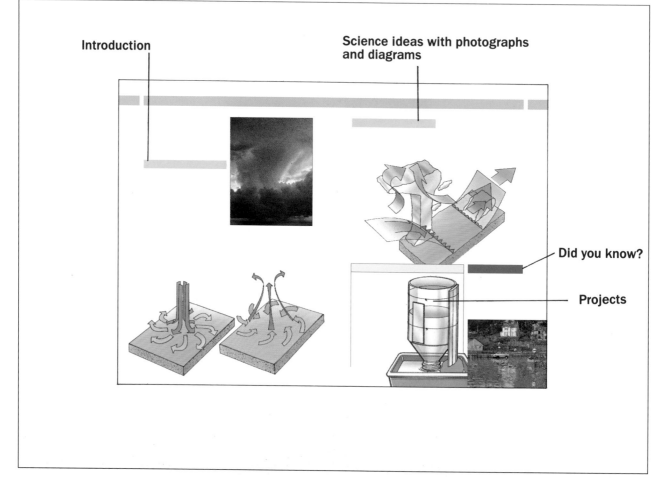

Introduction

Science ideas with photographs and diagrams

Did you know?

Projects

INTRODUCTION

Weather is news. Every day, millions of people tune into the weather forecast on television and radio or check the newspaper and telephone-line forecasts. Droughts, hurricanes, floods and storms are all news. Many people such as farmers, sailors, airline pilots, coastguards, builders and sportspeople all take a very keen interest in how the weather is likely to affect their lives. For example, it is important for farmers to know if the weather will be good for planting seeds, or for a sailor to know whether there will be dangerous storms at sea.

The weather also gets into the news because many scientists say the world's weather is changing and getting hotter. They think this is a result of increasing pollution.

This book is an introduction to the basic ideas about weather — why the wind blows, why it rains, why fog forms, why hurricanes develop and how the world's climate is changing.

Clouds take many shapes and forms.

Weather is the changes that take place in the air at any particular place. It is made up of things like rainfall, wind, temperature and clouds. In some places the weather changes often; in other places it stays the same day after day. The usual pattern of weather somewhere is called the climate of that place.

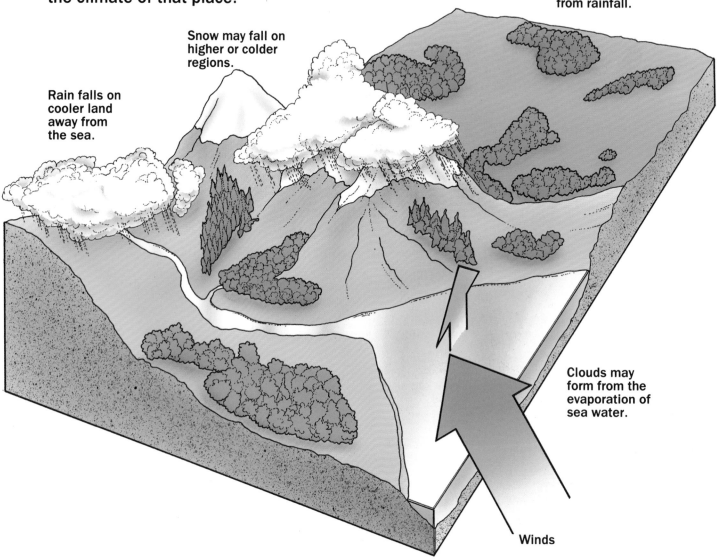

Rain often falls on high ground, such as hills or mountains, which tend to lift clouds higher.

Mountains can shelter some areas from rainfall.

Snow may fall on higher or colder regions.

Rain falls on cooler land away from the sea.

Clouds may form from the evaporation of sea water.

Winds

ATMOSPHERIC ENGINE

The Sun is the source of energy for changes in the atmosphere. Most of the Sun's rays pass all the way through the atmosphere and heat the land or the sea. The warm ground or sea then warms the air above it. This warm air at the bottom of the atmosphere then starts to rise.

When warm air rises, cooler, heavier air moves in to replace it. In turn, this cold air is warmed by the land or sea and also starts to rise. The process of warm air rising and cold air taking its place is called convection. It is the "engine" that drives the weather "machine".

Air is constantly warming and rising or cooling and descending. These movements cause changes in the atmosphere that lead to changes in the weather. For example, rising warm air may carry evaporated water with it. This water may then fall as rain.

ABOVE THE EARTH

The Earth is surrounded by a thick band of air called the atmosphere. The layer of air nearest the ground is known as the troposphere. This is where weather happens. The troposphere is about 11 kilometres high. It is the warmest layer of the atmosphere. But the air becomes cooler away from Earth's surface, and it is very cold at the top of the troposphere.

The atmosphere is made up of a mixture of gases: three-quarters is nitrogen, and most of the rest is oxygen. There are also tiny amounts of carbon dioxide and water vapour. It is this water vapour which creates the clouds that bring rain, snow and hail. Above the troposphere are further layers of the atmosphere extending for about 500 kilometres. Little or no weather occurs in these layers.

▷ In the upper atmosphere, the air is very thin. Auroras (the Northern and Southern Lights) are produced when radiation from the Sun hits the outer layers of the atmosphere.

▽ The clouds that can be seen from space are very rarely higher than the troposphere. The cloudless atmosphere above this is invisible.

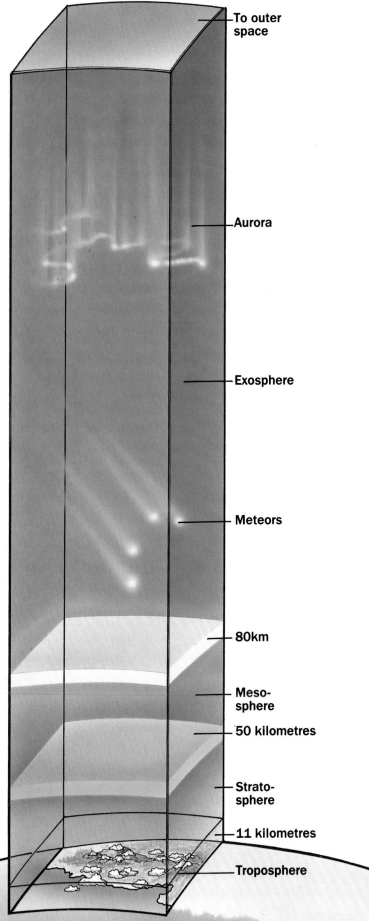

To outer space

Aurora

Exosphere

Meteors

80km

Meso-sphere

50 kilometres

Strato-sphere

11 kilometres

Troposphere

Temperature is the word we use to describe how hot or cold something is. Where we live and how we feel will change our idea of what is warm and what is cold. So to measure temperature we use a thermometer, which shows degrees Celsius (sometimes known as degrees centigrade).

▷ The North and South Poles are cold and always covered by snow and ice. The frozen surface makes life difficult for people and animals in these places. But snowmobiles make getting around easier.

▷ Camels are ideally suited for getting around in hot, dry deserts. They can go for long periods without food or water, and their thick, wiry hair protects them from the heat. People who live in deserts wear long, loose clothes.

FEWER RAYS

Different places on the Earth's surface receive different amounts of heat and light from the Sun. This is because the Sun's rays spread out more on the surface at the poles than at the Equator. As a result, places near the Equator are hotter than those near the poles.

1 In both polar regions (1 and 5), light is at its weakest.

2 The Sun's rays travel parallel to each other in straight lines.

3 Light is least spread out on the Earth's surface at the Equator.

4 Light is more spread out farther from the Equator.

5 Light rays at the poles (1 and 5) also have to travel farther through the atmosphere.

TEMPERATURE EXPERIMENTS

To measure the air temperature you need an ordinary, household thermometer. But you must keep it in a shaded place, like the box shown here. Cut out the shapes, taking care to use strong card. Put the thermometer inside the box, balanced on the supports. The flaps in the side of the box let air flow through. It is best to put flaps on both sides. Paint the box white. This will reflect away any direct sunlight.

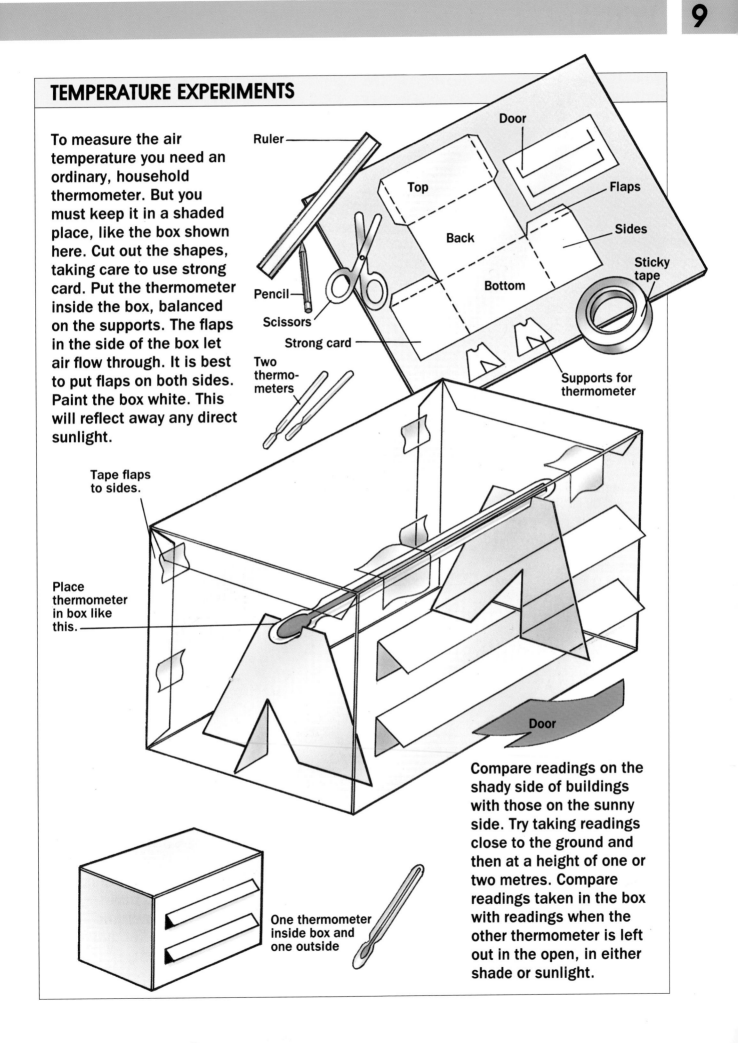

Ruler

Door

Top

Back

Flaps

Sides

Bottom

Sticky tape

Pencil

Scissors

Strong card

Two thermo-meters

Supports for thermometer

Tape flaps to sides.

Place thermometer in box like this.

Door

One thermometer inside box and one outside

Compare readings on the shady side of buildings with those on the sunny side. Try taking readings close to the ground and then at a height of one or two metres. Compare readings taken in the box with readings when the other thermometer is left out in the open, in either shade or sunlight.

Wind is moving air. The air around the Earth is always on the move, both across the surface and up and down in the atmosphere. Sometimes we can tell where the winds have come from. For example, dust from the Sahara Desert has settled in northern Europe. There are patterns of wind around the world.

WORLD'S WINDS

At the Equator, air is heated, causing it to rise. This creates low air pressure. On each side of the Equator — about 3,000 kilometres north and south — cool air sinks to the Earth's surface. This creates high air pressure. Winds blow from the high pressure to the low. Because the Earth is spinning, the winds also swirl round in the patterns shown below. The

winds around the Equator cause other wind patterns farther north and south. All this means that in many parts of the world there is one direction in which the wind usually blows.

▽ The steady, reliable winds once used by sailing ships making regular journeys are known as trade winds.

△ Strong winds can easily make trees bend. Stronger winds can cause a great deal of damage.

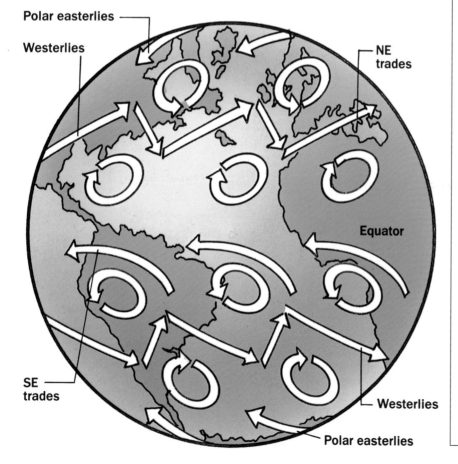

Polar easterlies

Westerlies

NE trades

Equator

SE trades

Westerlies

Polar easterlies

WIND PROJECT

To make a wind vane, fix two triangular pieces of card to a drinking straw (the tail piece should be larger than the head). Pin the straw to the end of a rubber-ended pencil. Fix the pencil into a hole in the bottom of a plastic bottle. The arrow will point to the direction from which the wind is blowing.

Wind speed is measured by an anemometer. This can be made in much the same way as a wind vane, but with four arms and with a counter added. Check how many times the anemometer turns in a fixed period of time — say 20 seconds.

BEAUFORT SCALE

In the early nineteenth century, Sir Francis Beaufort developed a system for judging wind speed. He wanted a guide to wind speed for use at sea. He made up a scale based on miles per hour, and at each point he gave the wind a number, a name, a speed and a description of its effects. His original descriptions were mostly related to the effects of wind on sailing ships. For example, at 2 on the scale a ship would travel at about 1 to 2 miles per hour.

The Beaufort scale has 13 points (0 to 12). Zero on the scale represents no wind at all, and 1 is a very slight breeze. At 5 on the scale, small branches on trees sway and paper blows about. Force 8 on the scale is a gale, and it is very difficult to walk against the wind.

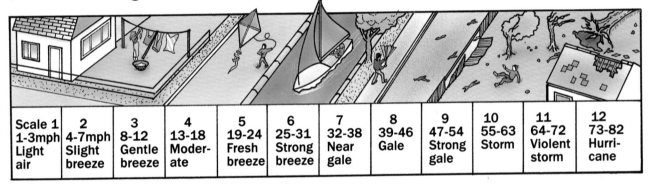

Scale 1 1-3mph Light air	2 4-7mph Slight breeze	3 8-12 Gentle breeze	4 13-18 Moder-ate	5 19-24 Fresh breeze	6 25-31 Strong breeze	7 32-38 Near gale	8 39-46 Gale	9 47-54 Strong gale	10 55-63 Storm	11 64-72 Violent storm	12 73-82 Hurri-cane

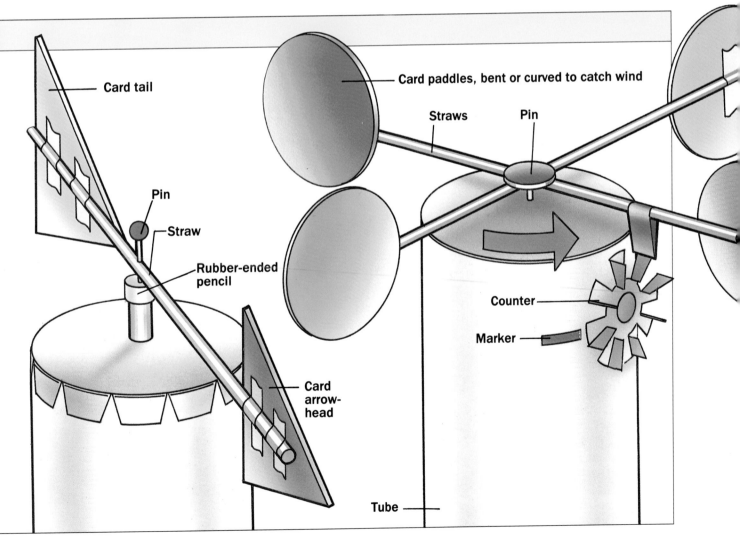

Card tail

Pin

Straw

Rubber-ended pencil

Card arrowhead

Tube

Card paddles, bent or curved to catch wind

Straws

Pin

Counter

Marker

Clouds are made up of millions of tiny droplets of water or ice. Pilots of aeroplanes inside clouds can see nothing but cloud. Being inside a cloud is like being in a very thick fog. Each cloud droplet is smaller than a grain of flour. The water droplets are so small and light that they can float in the air.

FORMATION OF CLOUDS

All air contains at least some water vapour. Water vapour is a gas. When air rises, it cools and the water vapour condenses (turns into tiny drops of water) to form clouds. Air may start to rise for various reasons. For example, in some places air is heated by the warm ground and so rises. In other places air rises to pass over hills and mountains. In other cases cold, heavy air pushes under warm air and forces it to rise.

△ Different types of cloud bring different types of weather. These cumulus clouds often indicate fine weather.

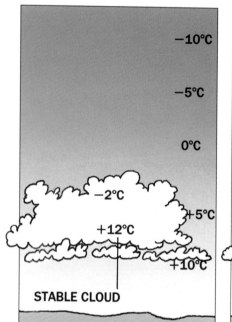

STABLE CLOUD

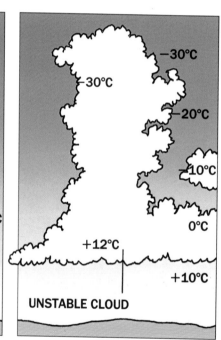

UNSTABLE CLOUD

▷ There are many types of cloud, and cloud names are often joined together. For example, a cumulonimbus is a cumulus that gives rain, or an altostratus is a high stratus.

Cumulus

△ As air rises it cools and the water vapour in it condenses to form clouds. When the atmosphere around the cloud is warmer than the cloud itself, only stable clouds are formed. A stratus cloud is a typical sort of stable cloud.

△ If the rising air that is forming a cloud is much warmer than the air around it, it rises to a considerable height. The cloud cools down, but it remains warmer than the surrounding air. A cumulonimbus cloud is of this type.

DID YOU KNOW?

There is an old saying that a red sky in the evening means good weather the next day. Meteorologists tell us that there is some evidence that this is true.

DIFFERENT SORTS OF CLOUD

Clouds vary in shape and in their height above the Earth. Clouds that look like cotton wool are called cumulus. They have flat bases and tops shaped like cauliflowers. Stratus are layers of cloud that look like even sheets, covering all or part of the sky. They are usually quite low in the air. Cirrus are thin wisps of cloud, high up in the atmosphere. They are made up of ice crystals. Clouds that give prolonged rain are called nimbostratus. The base of a cumulonimubs cloud is often low, but it may tower to great heights.

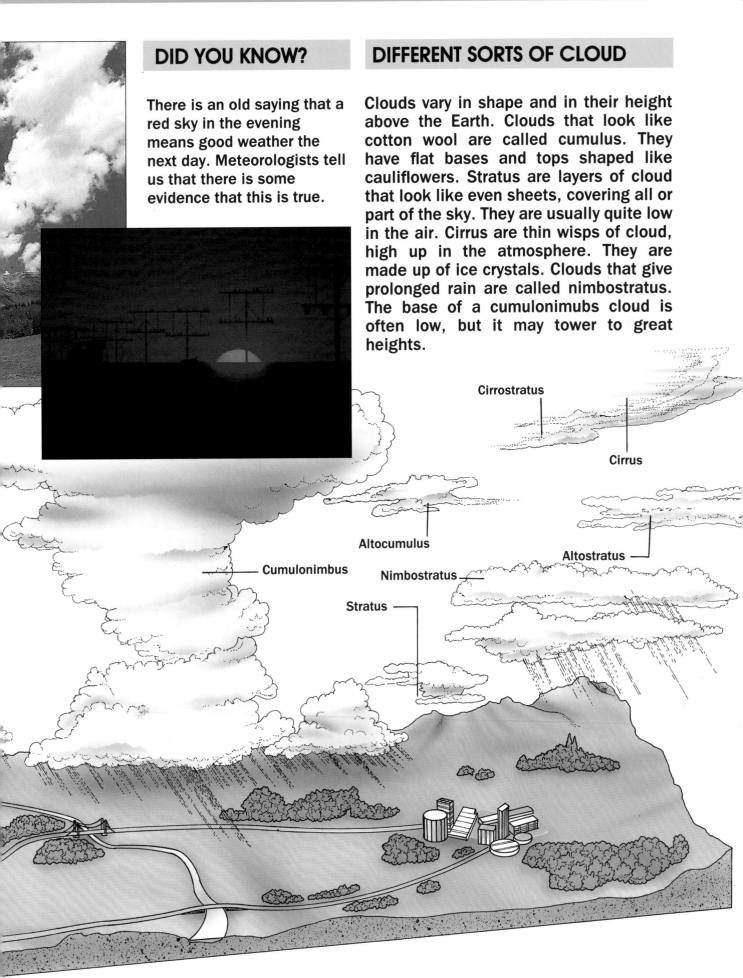

Cirrostratus

Cirrus

Altocumulus

Altostratus

Cumulonimbus

Nimbostratus

Stratus

Water is constantly on the move in a process called the water cycle. Winds pick up water vapour that has evaporated from the sea, and which forms clouds. When the clouds reach land, often the water falls as rain or snow. This drains into rivers and streams that flow back to the sea, and the process starts again.

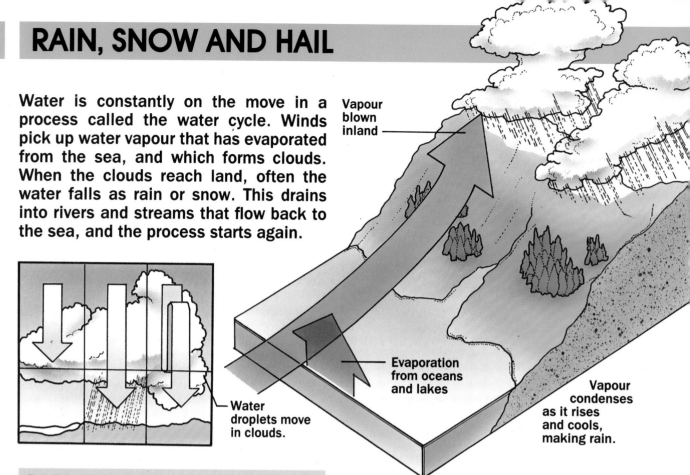

Vapour blown inland

Evaporation from oceans and lakes

Water droplets move in clouds.

Vapour condenses as it rises and cools, making rain.

RAIN AND SNOW

Rain or snow starts in clouds. The tiny droplets of water floating in a cloud stick to particles of dust, salt from ocean spray, or ice. The water droplets inside the cloud grow bigger and bump into each other to grow even more. Eventually, the droplets become too big and heavy to be held up in the air any longer, and they fall from the cloud as rain. If the temperature of the cloud is below freezing, the water vapour turns into ice crystals, which form snowflakes.

▽ Rain gives water for drinking, for farms and for factories. Too much leads to floods, too little brings drought.

▽ Snow can get very deep and cover a whole landscape. But in most parts of the world it soon melts to provide water.

HAIL

Hail falls only from tall cumulonimbus clouds. Inside the clouds there are very strong vertical air currents. Raindrops that form inside a cloud are carried up and down by these air currents. At the top of the cloud it is very cold and the raindrops freeze. Then, as they fall, more water sticks to them and freezes a layer at a time so that the frozen drops get bigger and bigger. They may travel up and down again many times inside the cloud. When the raindrop eventually falls it is a lump of ice called a hailstone.

▷ If a hailstone is cut in half, layers of ice can be seen. Large hailstones can cause a great amount of damage.

Layers on a hailstone

MAKE A RAIN GAUGE

Carefully cut the top from a flat-bottomed plastic bottle. Place the top upside down inside the cut-down bottle. Then seal it in place using sticky tape. Use a ruler to make a scale showing millimetres and stick it upright on one side of the bottle. You can use the gauge to find out how much rain falls in a day, week or month.

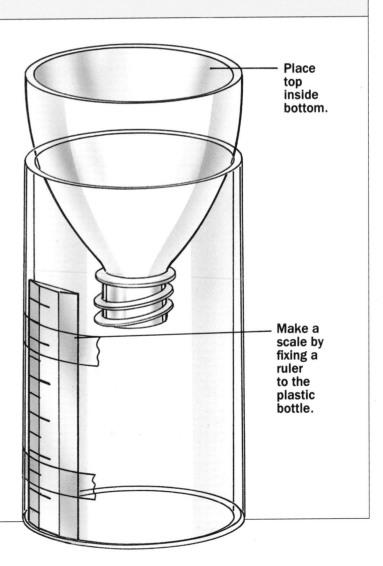

Place top inside bottom.

Make a scale by fixing a ruler to the plastic bottle.

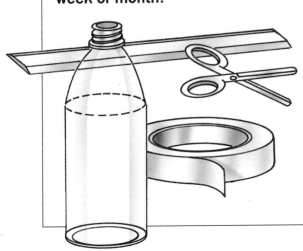

Fog, mist, dew and frost all form when water vapour in the air cools until it condenses (turns to water). This process is more or less the same as that by which clouds form. But with fog, mist, dew and frost the condensation takes place close to or on the ground. And it is often the ground itself that cools the air.

FOG

Fog often forms after sunset on fine days with clear skies and no wind, although it can form in many other conditions. The surface of the ground loses heat rapidly. As the ground cools, it cools the air that is in contact with it. The cool air is heavier than the surrounding air, so it tends to collect near the ground in hollows and in the bottoms of valleys. Eventually the water vapour in the air condenses into droplets, which form the fog. To weather forecasters the difference between fog and mist is that, with fog, visibility (how far it is possible to see) is less than 1,000 metres.

△ The tiny water droplets that make up fog are suspended in air close to the ground. This makes visibility a problem.

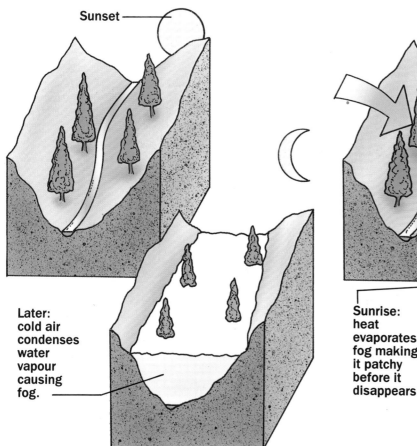

Sunset

Later: cold air condenses water vapour causing fog.

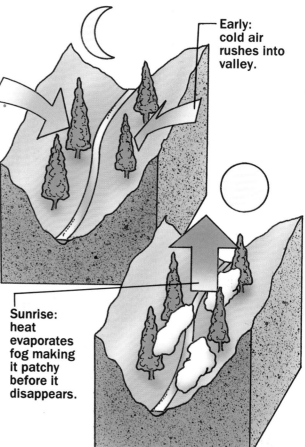

Early: cold air rushes into valley.

Sunrise: heat evaporates fog making it patchy before it disappears.

FROST AND DEW

On calm, clear nights, cold ground cools the air close to it. Water vapour in the air condenses on to cold surfaces, such as plants, forming large droplets of water called dew.

If the temperature of the ground is below freezing, then frost will form instead of dew. Cars, roads and plants may be covered by a white layer of frost. On windows, frost forms feathery crystals. Sometimes water vapour or rain freezes into a layer of clear slippery ice, particularly on roads. This is called black ice and is a very dangerous type of frost because drivers cannot see it.

▽ Frost can form very beautiful patterns in the landscape. It can also kill plants and make roads and paths slippery and dangerous.

FREEZING PROJECT

Water expands when it freezes. This is why water pipes can burst in cold weather. Fill a plastic bottle to the rim and put on the cap. Freeze it, and it will bulge or split. **Do not use a glass bottle.**

Before freezing

After freezing

The weight of the air in the atmosphere pressing down on the Earth is called air pressure. This pressure varies from place to place, and areas of pressure often move. Areas of high pressure (called anticyclones) bring fine weather. Areas of low pressure (called depressions) bring cloud and rain.

HIGHS AND LOWS

In anticyclones, in which air pressure is high, the air is slowly sinking towards the surface of the Earth. As the air descends it gets warmer and so can hold more water vapour. This means that the weather is usually fine. When the air reaches the surface, it spreads out and rotates clockwise (in the Northern Hemisphere) because of the Earth's rotation.

In depressions, in which air pressure is low, air rises. As it rises, it cools and so can hold less water vapour. As a result, clouds and rain are formed. The rotation of the Earth causes the air to rise in an anticlockwise spiral. The directions in which air spirals are reversed in the Southern Hemisphere.

△ When two masses of air meet, clouds form. Often the air masses are very different. If one is warm and wet and the other is cold and dry, dark clouds quickly form, often with rain, hail or thunder.

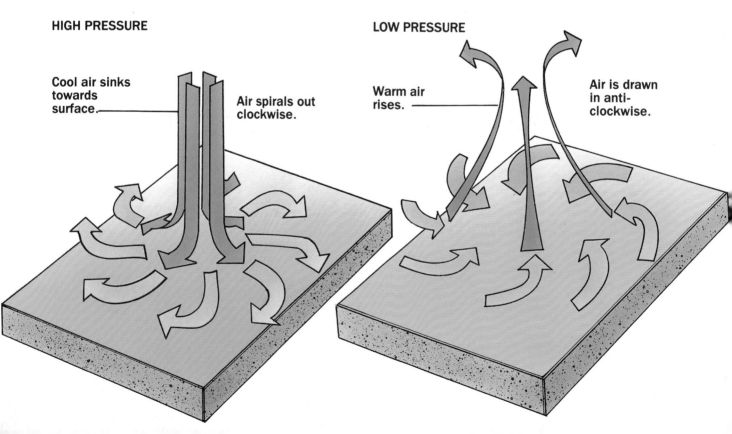

HIGH PRESSURE

Cool air sinks towards surface.

Air spirals out clockwise.

LOW PRESSURE

Warm air rises.

Air is drawn in anti-clockwise.

INSIDE A DEPRESSION

As the air in a depression swirls round, fronts move with it. Fronts are belts of cloud and rain where masses of warm air are rising over cold air. With a warm front, a mass of warm air catches up with a mass of cold air. The warm air rises quite slowly over the cold air, so the rain is often a light drizzle. With a cold front, cold air pushes underneath the warm air. The warm air rises rapidly, and there is often heavy rain or even thunderstorms. An occluded front is when one front catches up with another.

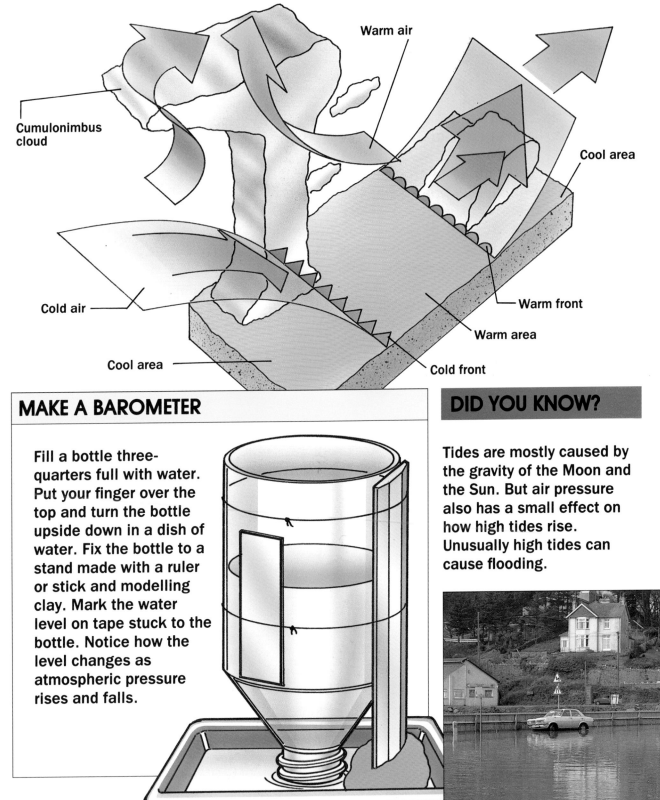

Warm air

Cumulonimbus cloud

Cool area

Cold air

Warm front

Warm area

Cool area

Cold front

MAKE A BAROMETER

Fill a bottle three-quarters full with water. Put your finger over the top and turn the bottle upside down in a dish of water. Fix the bottle to a stand made with a ruler or stick and modelling clay. Mark the water level on tape stuck to the bottle. Notice how the level changes as atmospheric pressure rises and falls.

DID YOU KNOW?

Tides are mostly caused by the gravity of the Moon and the Sun. But air pressure also has a small effect on how high tides rise. Unusually high tides can cause flooding.

Forecasts are made by collecting information from around the world. This information includes temperature, humidity, sunshine, wind speed and direction, air pressure and rainfall. Computers process the information into special maps called synoptic charts. These are used to predict the weather.

GATHERING INFORMATION

Information for weather forecasting comes from many sources. Weather stations record information at ground level, and automatic weather stations send back data from remote places. Satellites collect data such as temperature and cloud cover in parts of the atmosphere we cannot see. Weather balloons are sent 20 kilometres up into the air every day. They carry radio transmitters and send details about the temperature and humidity of the atmosphere at different heights. Weather ships make reports on conditions at sea. Radar is used to track the progress of rain across the country, and produces maps that show the amount. Special aircraft fitted with instruments measure atmospheric changes.

△ Weather forecasters are like detectives. They use clues about the weather in order to give television forecasts.

▽ Meteorologists use the information from a synoptic chart to scientifically predict the next day's weather.

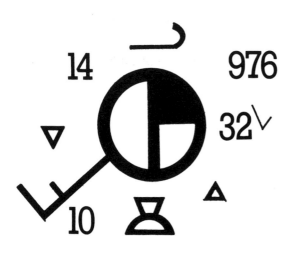

△ Symbols like this show the weather in a particular place; for example, the "F" shows where the wind is coming from.

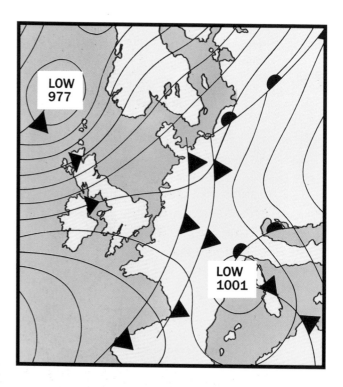

USING THE FORECAST

Millions of people look at or listen to television, radio and newspaper forecasts every day. For some people this is simply to know what to wear next day. However, many other people or organizations study the weather forecast carefully. For example, farmers need to know the best time to harvest their crops. Supermarket managers need to know if the demand for ice cream and soft drinks is likely to increase. Airlines can save money and fuel by routing aeroplanes so that they are not flying against wind.

▷ Knowing the positions of the main cloud formations over the Earth helps forecasters to understand the weather.

▷ Satellites have helped to make modern weather observation and forecasting much more accurate.

▽ Computers track and record the movement of weather systems around the world. This is important in stormy areas.

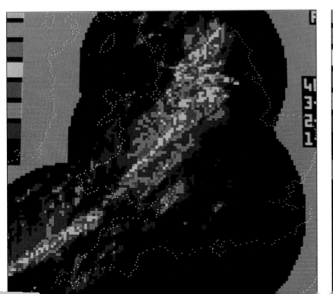

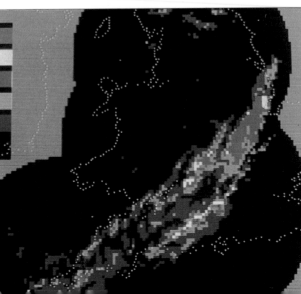

Extreme weather can be very dangerous. Every year it brings disaster to many places around the world. The weather can cause millions of pounds worth of damage, and it may injure people or even kill them. As forecasting and planning improve, the worst effects of severe weather can sometimes be avoided.

HURRICANES

Hurricanes are extremely destructive storms. They usually form over warm oceans in areas where winds from opposite directions meet. Swirls of air form. These begin to create a spiral. Gradually the air in the spiral moves faster and faster, until it reaches speeds of up to 300 kilometres per hour. The wind is strong enough to demolish houses and whip up huge waves. The centre, or "eye", of a hurricane is a calm area surrounded by violent winds.

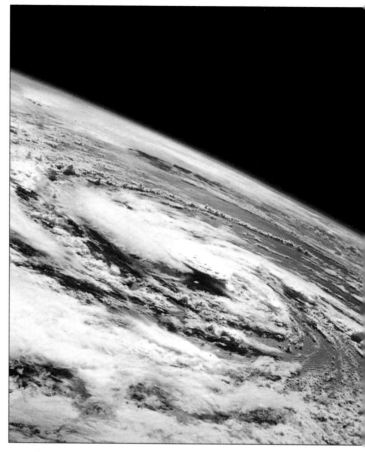

△ Hurricanes form over the Atlantic Ocean. The same sort of wind over the Pacific Ocean is called a typhoon.

▽ Tornadoes are most common in the central parts of the United States. They suck up many things in their paths.

TORNADOES

Tornadoes form over land and are often more violent than hurricanes. They start when hot, damp air meets cool, dry air and rises extremely fast. A funnel of cloud forms, which can be up to 200 metres high. Winds in tornadoes blow at up to 500 kilometres per hour. Tornadoes are usually a few hundred metres in diameter, and swirl around a centre which is about 100 metres wide. They last for between 15 minutes and five hours, and travel between 30 and 300 kilometres. They can destroy almost everything in their paths. When tornadoes pass over water, they suck it into the air to form a waterspout. In large tornadoes, small frogs, fish and other animals can be swept up into the air.

THUNDER & LIGHTNING

There are violent air currents inside cumulonimbus clouds. These currents cause ice crystals to crash into each other. This creates friction and splitting, which cause static electricity. Positive charges build up at the top of a cloud, and negative ones at the bottom. The ground has a positive charge. The difference between charges gets bigger until lightning sparks across the gap.

Lightning almost instantly heats the air in its path to about 30,000°C. This causes the air to expand very fast. Thunder is the sound of the hot air expanding.

▽ Lightning can damage buildings and injure or kill people. Lightning takes the shortest path to the ground.

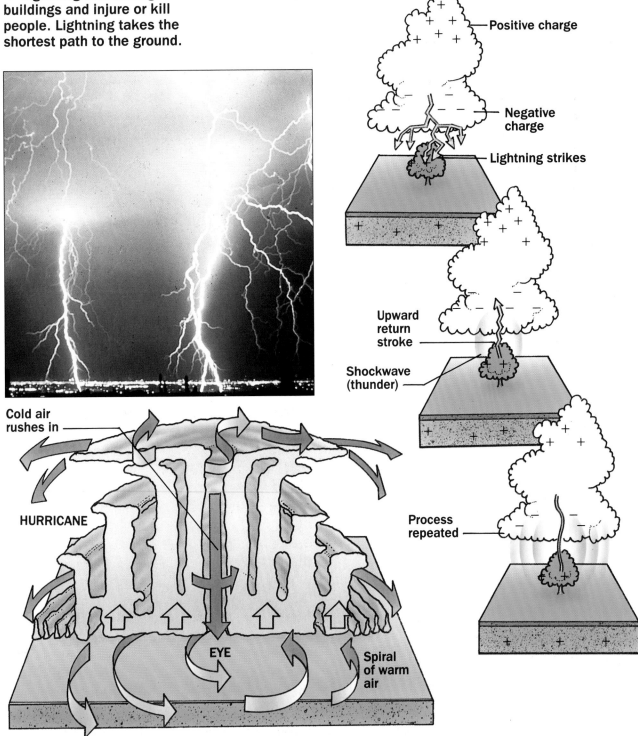

Positive charge

Negative charge

Lightning strikes

Upward return stroke

Shockwave (thunder)

Process repeated

Cold air rushes in

HURRICANE

EYE

Spiral of warm air

In many parts of the world, the main type of weather that occurs changes during the course of the year (as shown in the four pictures below). Each period with particular type of weather is known as a season. Seasons have a direct effect on plant and animal life; for example, plants start to grow in spring seasons.

ALL THE YEAR ROUND

Seasons are the result of the tilt of the Earth as it orbits round the Sun. At one end of the Earth's orbit, the North Pole is pointing towards the Sun and the Northern Hemisphere has its hot summer and the Southern Hemisphere has its cold winter. Six months later, the opposite is true. In between, the weather changes during spring and autumn.

These seasons happen because the Sun's rays are spread more thinly in parts of the world tilted away from the Sun (in winter). Also, the length of each day is shorter. The opposite is true when that part of the Earth is tilted towards the Sun in summer. (Compare this to the reason why the poles are cold on page 8.)

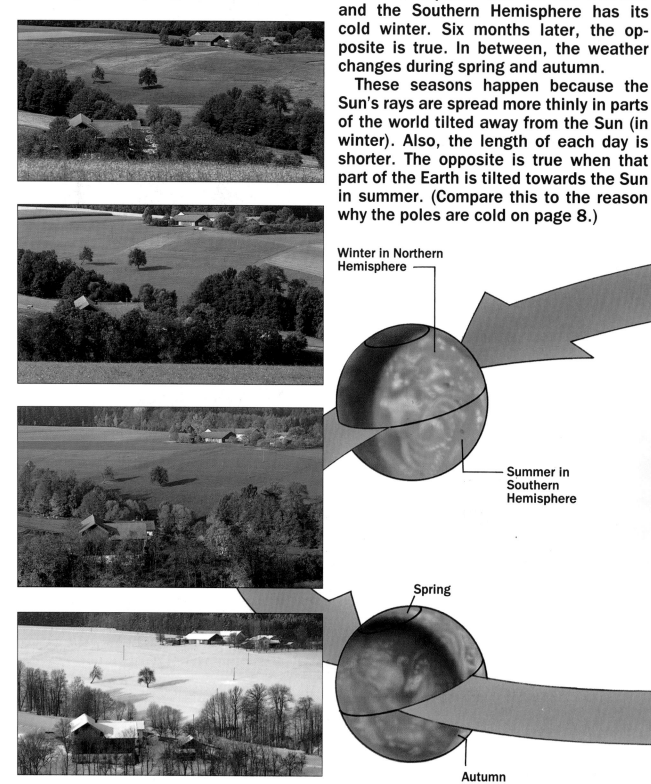

Winter in Northern Hemisphere

Summer in Southern Hemisphere

Spring

Autumn

DIFFERENT PLACES

The North and South Poles have only two seasons, which are six months of winter followed by six months of summer. Places in between the Equator and the poles usually have spring and autumn as well as summer and winter. Places near the Equator really have only one season, which is like summer. This is because the Sun is always high in the sky. In some places, particularly southern Asia, the seasons change very quickly. The wind blows from the north-east for six months then, within a day, it can turn around and blow from the south-west. These seasonal winds are called monsoons. The monsoon from the south-west brings a season of heavy rain.

△ The rain brought by the south-westerly monsoon winds in Asia is vital for rice growing. But the rain can also cause rivers to overflow and flood the surrounding land.

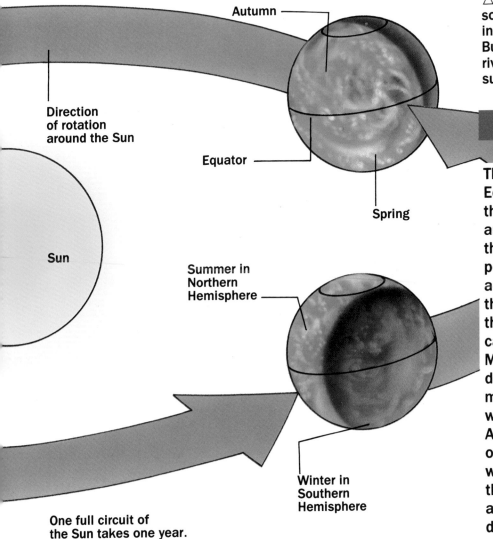

Autumn

Direction of rotation around the Sun

Equator

Sun

Spring

Summer in Northern Hemisphere

Winter in Southern Hemisphere

One full circuit of the Sun takes one year.

DID YOU KNOW?

The farther away from the Equator you get, the longer the days are in the summer and the shorter they are in the winter. Near to the poles, the Sun never sets at all for nearly six months in the summer. This is why these areas are sometimes called the Land of the Midnight Sun. Also, the Sun does not rise for several months in the middle of winter. At the Arctic and Antarctic Circles, there are only two or three days on which the Sun never sets. At the Equator, there is hardly any variation in the length of days all year.

Each part of the Earth tends to have certain types of weather. These range from generally hot, dry weather in deserts to mostly cold and snowy weather at the poles. The pattern of weather in each place is called its climate. For example, the west of Europe has a generally mild climate, with few extremes of weather.

▽ Climate has a big effect on plants. These maps show the main types of vegetation in different areas.

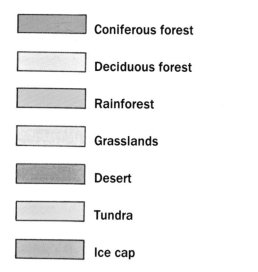

Coniferous forest

Deciduous forest

Rainforest

Grasslands

Desert

Tundra

Ice cap

DIFFERENT CLIMATES

Geographers divide the world into areas with different types of climate. The climate in each place depends on very many factors. These include how far the place is from the Equator, how far it is from the sea, and how high it is.

An example of two places with different climates is Glasgow in Scotland and Moscow in the Soviet Union. These cities are roughly the same distance north of the Equator. But their climates are very different. Moscow is much colder in winter and much hotter in summer. There is a difference in climate because Glasgow is very close to the sea, whereas Moscow is hundreds of kilometres inland. Places like Glasgow, which are near the sea, are said to have a maritime climate. In a maritime climate, temperatures do not vary much throughout the year. Places like Moscow have a continental climate, with yearly extremes of temperature.

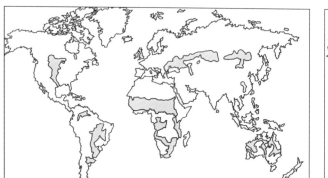

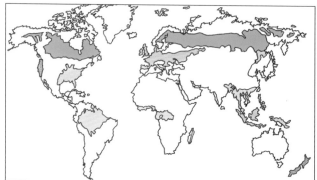

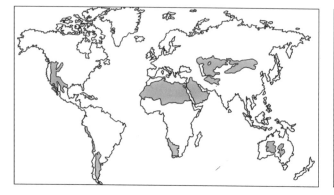

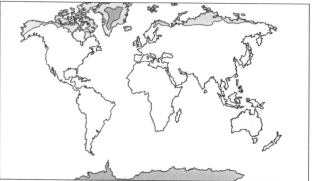

ALTITUDE AND CLIMATE

Climate changes with altitude (height) in much the same way as it changes as you travel away from the Equator towards the poles. Temperatures decrease as altitude gets higher. And as the temperature changes, so does the rest of the climate and the vegetation. So on high mountains close to the Equator it is possible to move through several climates before reaching snow. Above this, climate is much like that at the poles!

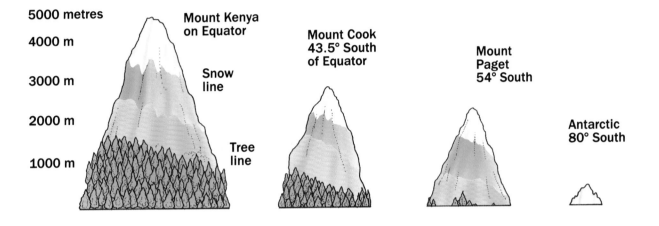

CURRENTS AND CLIMATE

Warm and cool ocean currents affect the climate of coastal areas. This happens particularly if the winds are blowing from the sea to the shore and carrying the sea's influence inland. Currents that flow towards the poles are warmer than the surrounding water, and so are called warm currents. Currents that flow towards the Equator are usually colder than the surrounding water, and so are called cold currents. Warm currents have most effect in winter, when they make coasts warmer than areas farther inland. Cold currents have most effect in summer, when they cool the coasts.

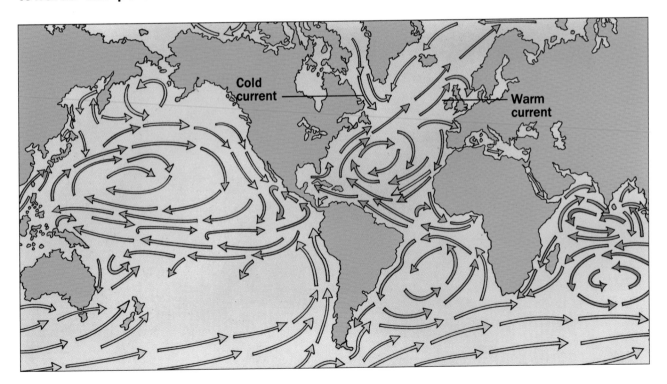

Accurate records of the weather only started about 200 years ago. This makes it difficult to tell if the world's weather is changing. Most scientists think that it is, but they disagree about what things cause the changes and how big the changes are. Many people believe that pollution is to blame.

THE GREENHOUSE EFFECT

The Greenhouse Effect is the name given to a suspected rise in temperatures around the world. This rise would be caused by the increasing amount of carbon dioxide and other "greenhouse gases" — such as methane and nitrous oxide — in the atmosphere. These gases come mainly from some power stations which burn coal or oil, vehicle exhausts and the burning of large areas of the world's rain forests. The Greenhouse Effect could lead to a rise in sea levels as polar ice caps melt, as well as very unpredictable weather.

△ There has been a 25 per cent increase in the amount of carbon dioxide in the atmosphere. This may be having a dangerous effect on the world's weather.

▽ Greenhouse gases in the atmosphere act like the glass in a greenhouse. They allow the Sun's rays through to heat the Earth, but trap some of the heat that could escape.

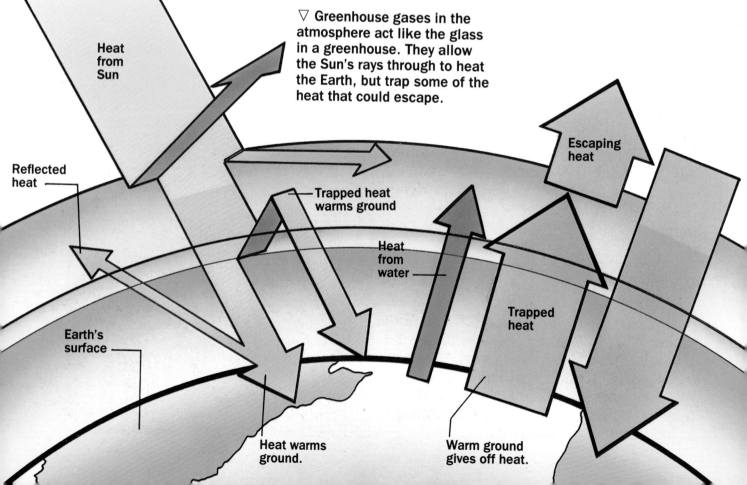

Heat from Sun

Reflected heat

Trapped heat warms ground

Heat from water

Escaping heat

Trapped heat

Earth's surface

Heat warms ground.

Warm ground gives off heat.

THE OZONE LAYER

The ozone layer is a cloud of a gas called ozone (a form of oxygen) about 25 kilometres up in the atmosphere. It is very important because it keeps out some of the harmful ultraviolet rays from the Sun. It also helps to stop the Earth getting too cold. Scientists first discovered a thinning in the ozone layer over Antarctica. Since then, people have found that the same thing is happening over the North Pole. These "holes" are believed to be caused mainly by gases called chlorofluorocarbons (or CFCs) escaping from aerosols, refrigerators and other products.

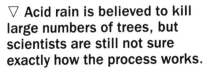

◁ Satellites can take pictures of "holes" in the ozone layer (marked in blue) which computers turn into false-colour photographs.

▽ Acid rain is believed to kill large numbers of trees, but scientists are still not sure exactly how the process works.

ACID RAIN

Acid rain was first reported in Scandinavia in the 1960s. Scientists noticed that fish were dying in lakes and rivers because the water had become very acidic. The water had been made acidic by acid carried in rain.

The acid in rain comes mostly from sulphur dioxide and nitrogen oxides that are produced by burning coal and oil. A large quantity of these gases comes from power stations. The gases are carried into the atmosphere and then spread over a wide area by the wind. They dissolve in the rain water, and turn it into sulphuric and nitric acids. These acids damage plants, crops and buildings.

Most of Northern Europe was covered by thick sheets of ice about 20,000 years ago. This was the last ice age. Since then, the climate has become warmer and much of the ice has melted. There have been several ice ages. We are now in a warm period between two ice ages, which could last 40,000 years.

Glacier

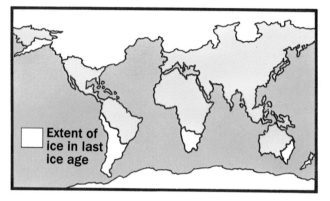

Extent of ice in last ice age

The weather 2,000 years ago was much warmer than now. This meant, for example, that grapes could be grown in Britain, which was ruled by the Romans at the time. Between 1600 and 1800 the world had a "little ice age" when glaciers and sheets of ice grew thicker. It became quite common in winter to see people skating on large rivers that never freeze over now. They even held "frost fairs" in the middle of such rivers.

Between 1800 and 1900, the world's weather began to warm up again. This meant ice sheets became thinner and glaciers in Europe began to retreat. As the ice melted, the bodies of explorers who had fallen into crevasses in the ice were gradually revealed. Since 1900, average temperatures seem to have continued rising. Sometimes events can have an effect on the weather. In 1883, when the volcano Krakatoa exploded, dust stayed in the air for 3 years. This had a temporary cooling effect, because the dust blocked some heat from the Sun.

Krakatoa exploding

Acid rain
Rain that is acidic because it contains dissolved sulphur dioxide and other substances. It causes damage to trees and buildings.

Air mass
A volume of warm, cold, moist or dry air in the atmosphere.

Air pressure
The weight of the Earth's atmosphere pressing down on the Earth's surface (or any other surface).

Anemometer
An instrument that is used for measuring wind speed.

Anticyclone
An area of high pressure in the Earth's atmosphere.

Barometer
An instrument that is used for measuring air pressure.

Climate
The average weather in a particular place on Earth.

Cold front
A boundary between colder and warmer air, where the colder air is replacing the warmer air.

Condensation
The process in which water vapour turns into tiny drops of water as it cools below the dew point.

Convection
The process by which light, hot air rises and is replaced by cooler, denser air.

Depression
An area of low pressure in the Earth's atmosphere.

Dew
Droplets of moisture that condense on cold surfaces. This often occurs early in the morning.

Dew point
The temperature at which water vapour in the air condenses into droplets.

Front
A boundary where a mass of warm air meets a mass of cold air.

Frost
Ice crystals frozen on to a cold surface.

Humidity
The amount of moisture in the air.

Isobars
Lines on a weather map that join places with the same air pressure.

Lightning
An electrical spark that jumps from cloud to cloud during storms, or from a cloud to the ground.

Meteorology
The science of studying the weather.

Precipitation
A general name for any type of water falling from the sky, e.g., rain, hail, sleet, snow and drizzle.

Stratosphere
The layer of the atmosphere between 15 and 50 kilometres above the Earth.

Warm front
The boundary between warmer air and colder air, where the warmer air is replacing the colder air.

Wind vane
An instrument that is used to indicate wind direction.

Photographic Credits:
Cover and pages 7, 14 right, 16-17, 19 and 25: Spectrum Colour Library; pages 5, 8 top and 12-13: Frank Lane Picture Agency; pages 8 bottom, 10, 17, 18, 21 top, 21 middle, 22 top, 23, 24 all, 28 and 29 bottom: Zefa; pages 13, 20, 22 bottom, 29 top and 30 top: Robert Harding Picture Library; page 14 left: Panos Pictures; page 15: The Hutchison Library; page 21 bottom left and bottom right: National Meteorological Library; page 30 bottom: Mary Evans Picture Library.